FREE DVD

MW00770115

From Stress to Success DVD from Trivium Test Prep

Dear Customer,

Thank you for purchasing from Trivium Test Prep! Whether you're a new teacher or looking to advance your career, we're honored to be a part of your journey.

To show our appreciation (and to help you relieve a little of that test-prep stress), we're offering a **FREE *ATI TEAS VI Test Tips DVD*** by Trivium Test Prep. Our DVD includes 35 test preparation strategies that will help keep you calm and collected before and during your big exam. All we ask is that you email us your feedback and describe your experience with our product. Amazing, awful, or just so-so: we want to hear what you have to say!

To receive your **FREE *ATI TEAS VI Test Tips DVD***, please email us at 5star@triviumtestprep.com. Include "Free 5 Star" in the subject line and the following information in your email:

1. The title of the product you purchased.

2. Your rating from 1 – 5 (with 5 being the best).

3. Your feedback about the product, including how our materials helped you meet your goals and ways in which we can improve our products.

4. Your full name and shipping address so we can send your **FREE *ATI TEAS VI Test Tips DVD***.

If you have any questions or concerns please feel free to contact us directly at 5star@triviumtestprep.com.

Thank you, and good luck with your studies!

---

* Please note that the free DVD is <u>not included</u> with this book. To receive the free DVD, please follow the instructions above.

ATI TEAS Flash Cards

TEAS 6 Test Prep Including Over 400 Flash Cards for the Test of Essential Academic Skills Exam, Sixth Edition

TABLE OF CONTENTS

INTRODUCTION

Congratulations on your decision to join the field of nursing—few other professions are so rewarding! By purchasing this book, you've already taken the first step towards succeeding in your career. The next step is to do well on the ATI Test of Essential Academic Skills (TEAS) VI, which will require you to demonstrate knowledge of high school–level reading, writing, math, and science.

ABOUT THE ATI TEAS VI

The ATI TEAS VI is three hours and twenty-nine minutes long and is divided into the following sections:

SUBJECT	SUB-AREAS	TIME LIMIT
Reading 53 questions: paragraph and passage comprehension and informational source comprehension	Key ideas and details (22)	64 minutes
	Craft and structure (14)	
	Integration of knowledge and ideas (11)	
	Pre-test questions (6, unscored)	
Mathematics 36 questions: numbers and operations, measurement, data interpretation, and algebra	Numbers and algebra (23)	54 minutes
	Measurement and data (9)	
	Pre-test questions (4, unscored)	

SUBJECT	SUB-AREAS	TIME LIMIT
Science 53 questions: scientific reasoning, human body science, life science, Earth science, and physical science	Human anatomy and physiology (32) Life and physical sciences (8) Scientific reasoning (7) Pre-test questions (6, unscored)	63 minutes
English and Language Arts 28 questions: grammar, punctuation, spelling, word meaning, and sentence structure	Conventions of standard English (9) Knowledge of language (9) Vocabulary acquisition (6) Pre-test questions (4, unscored)	28 minutes
Total: 170 questions	150 scored, 20 unscored	3 hours 29 minutes

There are a total of 170 questions on the TEAS; however twenty of them are unscored, pre-test questions and used only by the test makers to gather information. That means 150 of the questions you answer will count toward your score. Keep in mind that you will not know which questions will be unscored, so you must answer all of the questions on the exam.

If you take the online version of the TEAS, you will receive your score immediately after the test. If you take the paper-and-pencil version, ATI will score your exam within forty-eight hours of receiving it from the testing site. Your scores are automatically sent to the schools you selected when you registered for the exam. You must contact the administrators of the exam, the Assessment Technologies Institute (ATI), to send your scores to any other programs.

Scoring

You cannot pass or fail the TEAS exam. Instead, you will receive a score report that details the number of questions you answered correctly in each section and also gives your percentile rank, which shows how you did in comparison with other test-takers. Each school has its own entrance requirements, so be sure to check the requirements of the institutions you want to attend so you can set appropriate goals for yourself.

Administration and Test Day

The TEAS is administered by the Assessment Technologies Institute (ATI) at testing centers nationwide. To register for the exam, refer to the ATI website. You may take a computer-administered or pencil-and-paper test. There is no difference other than method of administration. Choose the format you are most comfortable with, but keep in mind that if you take the computer-administered version, you will receive your scores immediately.

On test day, arrive early and be sure to bring government-issued, photo identification; two No. 2 pencils; and your ATI login information. Personal belongings, cell phones, and other electronic, photographic, recording, or listening devices are not permitted in the testing center. Most testing centers offer lockers to secure your personal items, but it is a good idea to check beforehand with the facility. Calculators and scratch paper will be provided. There is a ten-minute break after the mathematics section. For the most up-to-date details on what to expect on test day, refer to the ATI website.

ABOUT TRIVIUM TEST PREP

Trivium Test Prep uses industry professionals with decades' worth of knowledge in their fields, proven with degrees and honors in law, medicine, business, education, the military, and more, to produce high quality test prep books for students.

Our study guides are specifically designed to increase any student's score. Our books are also shorter and more concise than typical study guides, so you can increase your score while significantly decreasing your study time.

ANATOMY AND PHYSIOLOGY

blood pressure

capillaries

Blood pressure is the force exerted on the vessels of the cardiovascular system as blood is pumped through the body.

Capillaries are the smallest blood vessels in the cardiovascular system. The thin network of vessels serves as the site of material exchange between arteries delivering blood and veins returning blood to the heart.

pulmonary ventilation

bronchiole

larynx

Pulmonary ventilation, or breathing, is the process of air filling the lungs during inspiration (inhalation) and releasing air from the lungs to the atmosphere during expiration (exhalation).

Bronchioles are small divisions of the bronchus, or air passage, found within the lungs. They connect to alveoli and transport gases in and out of the lungs during respiration.

The larynx is a hollow organ located in the neck on top of the trachea. In humans, the larynx contains vocal cords. As air passes over the larynx during respiration, the cords vibrate and create sound that can be manipulated to make speech.

chyme

bile

colon

Chyme is a mixture of partially digested food and digestive juices that forms in the stomach and is passed through to the small intestine for further digestion.

Bile is an acidic fluid that is produced by the liver and stored in the gall bladder. Bile aids in the breakdown of fat macronutrients during digestion.

The colon is a part of the large intestine that connects the cecum to the rectum. The colon is the largest part of the large intestine and is primarily responsible for water absorption and waste preparation.

nephron

spermatogenesis

menstrual cycle

Nephrons are small, fine tubes in the kidney that create urine and filter waste and other substances out of the blood.

Spermatogenesis is the process of sperm development in males. Spermatogonia, which are sperm stem cells, give rise to
spermatocytes in the seminiferous tubules within the testes.

The menstrual cycle occurs in human females as well as other female primates. It is the process of ovulation (the release of the egg into the fallopian tube) and menstruation, which is the shedding of the egg and uterine lining in the event fertilization does not occur.

somatic nervous system

medulla oblongata

visceral muscles

The somatic nervous system is a part of the peripheral nervous system and serves to control voluntary movement of the skeletal and muscle systems.

The medulla oblongata is a portion of the hindbrain that connects the brain to the spinal cord and is primarily responsible for regulation of autonomic bodily functions.

Visceral (smooth) muscles are tissues found inside veins and arteries, the stomach, and other internal organs. These muscles involuntarily contract to move blood, food, or other substances from one place to another. They are so named because of the lack of striations, or bands, found in other muscles.

sarcomere

sesamoid bone

appendicular skeleton

The sarcomere is comprised of both thick and thin filaments and is the basic unit found in myofibrils, which are the elongated organelles found within striated muscle tissue. As the muscles contract, the thick filaments slide by the thin filaments, thus shortening the myofibrils and causing muscle contraction.

A sesamoid bone is a small, rounded bone or nodule that is found within a tendon where the tendon passes over a joint. The patella, or kneecap, is the largest example of a sesamoid bone in the human body.

The appendicular skeleton is the division of the skeletal system that contains the bones of the appendages, or limbs, as well as the pectoral and pelvic girdles that attach to the axial skeleton.

trophic hormones

melatonin

inflammation

Trophic hormones are hormones that are produced in order to stimulate other glands to produce hormones. Most trophic hormones are produced by the anterior pituitary gland.

Melatonin is a hormone produced by the pineal glands in order to control sleep and wake cycles.

Inflammation is a nonspecific response to pathogens and injured cells. Localized tissue releases histamines that raise the temperature and blood flow to the target area, which triggers more white blood cells to enter the area in order to repair it.

antibodies

hypodermis

melanocytes

Antibodies are proteins produced by plasma that bind to the antigen protein found on the surface of pathogens. Once attached, the pathogen becomes neutralized and phago-cytes are stimulated to ingest the target cell.

The hypodermis is a deep layer of skin that stores fat, which provides insulation and support for the body.

Melanocytes are skin cells that produce melanin in order to protect the skin from UV radiation through sun exposure. The melanin pigment also gives skin its color.

thoracic duct

tonsils

atria

The thoracic duct collects lymph from the majority of the human body, then drains lymph into the bloodstream.

Tonsils are lymphatic nodules located in or near the pharynx. The human body has five tonsils which store *T*-cells and *B*-cells and aid the body in response to infection.

the chamber of the heart that receives blood from the lungs or other parts of the body

systole

external respiration

pleura

the contraction phase of the heartbeat, during which the heart ventricles force out blood into the lungs or to the body

the exchange of gases that occurs in the lungs at the alveoli

the delicate membrane that covers and lines the human lungs

peristalsis

absorption

esophagus

the muscular contractions that push food from one point to another within the digestive tract

the process of digested food moving into the bloodstream for cellular respiration

the part of the digestive tract that transports food from the throat to the stomach by contracting its muscular walls

sphincter

ureter

vas deferens

a circular muscle that, when relaxed, allows materials to pass through for excretion

a thin, muscular tube that transports urine from the kidney to the bladder

the long tube in the male reproductive system that serves as a pathway for sperm to travel to the urethra and mix with nutrients and fluids to form semen

ectoderm

synapse

cerebrum

the outermost germ layer of a human embryo, which eventually gives rise to the nervous system, skin, and sensory organs

---

the site of neuron communication between two cells, which permits one neuron to send an impulse to the next neuron

---

the dominant portion of the forebrain that is responsible for complex thinking, coordination of movement, and memory storage

myosin

isometric contraction

bursae

the protein found in the thick filament of sarcomeres that causes muscle contraction

the type of muscle contraction that causes increased muscle tension but does not result in skeletal movement

the fluid-filled sacs located in joint cavities that serve to cushion bone and reduce friction between a joint's moving parts

periosteum

thyroid

neurosecretion

the thin outer surface of a bone that contains an outer fibrous layer and an inner osteogenic layer

the endocrine gland located in the larynx that regulates metabolism in the human body

the secretion produced by nerve cells in order to stimulate the production and release of hormones in response to neural signals

memory cell

acquired immunity

follicle

the type of *B*-cell that stores information for producing antibodies in an immune response

the type of immunity that the body gains over time and exposure to specific antigens found on the surface of pathogens

the sac-like structure found within the dermis that produces hair

ceruminous gland

spleen

lymph

the gland that produces wax in order to protect the ear canal from foreign pathogens and other invaders

the abdominal organ that filters blood and produces white blood cells to help fight infection

the clear fluid that carries white blood cells throughout the body

What is the difference between the pulmonary circuit and the systemic circuit in the human cardiovascular system?

What is the purpose of the human cardiovascular system?

How does blood move through a four-chambered heart in a closed circulatory system?

In humans, the pulmonary circuit moves from the lungs to the heart in the pulmonary circuit, where it becomes oxygenated. Oxygenated blood then moves from the heart to the rest of the body's tissues via the systemic circuit.

The cardiovascular system transports oxygen and nutrients to body tissues, and carries carbon dioxide and wastes from body tissues for eventual excretion.

Blood flows from the right atrium to the right ventricle as the heart beats, opening the tricuspid valve and allowing blood to flow through. The right ventricle pumps the blood into the lungs for oxygenation. Oxygenated blood then returns to the heart and enters the left atrium before entering the left ventricle to be pumped to the rest of the body.

What is the primary organ of
the cardiovascular system,
and what is its function?

What are the stages of the cardiac cycle?

What occurs during the process
of respiration?

The heart, which is an organ composed of cardiac muscle, is the primary organ of the cardiovascular system. Its primary function is to pump blood throughout the body through a series of
contractions and relaxations.

The cardiac cycle consists of systole, which is the contraction of the heart that moves blood out of the ventricles, and diastole, which is the relaxation of the heart that allows blood to refill the atria.

During respiration, the body intakes oxygen from the atmosphere in order to break down glucose and provide energy to the body. Carbon dioxide, a byproduct of this process, is expelled after the exchange of gases. In humans, this process takes place in the lungs.

What is the function of the diaphragm in human respiration?

What role do alveoli play in gas exchange in the lungs?

How are the cardiovascular system and respiratory system interconnected?

The diaphragm is a muscle that separates the lungs from the abdomen in the thoracic cavity. During inhalation—the first phase of respiration—the diaphragm contracts to open up the thoracic cavity and allows air to flow into the lungs. During exhalation, the diaphragm relaxes and allows air to flow out of the lungs into the atmosphere.

Alveoli, which are air sacs found at the end of the smallest bronchioles branching throughout the lungs, contain a membrane that is only one cell thick. This thin layer allows oxygen to be diffused into the blood and carbon dioxide to be diffused out of the blood.

The respiratory system delivers oxygen to the lungs, where it diffuses in the blood and is sent to the heart to be transported to the rest of the body. The lungs also remove carbon dioxide from the blood that is pumped to the heart and expel the gas from the body through exhalation.

What is the difference between chemical
and mechanical digestion?

What is the role of accessory
organs in digestion?

Why is the human digestive system
considered a complete digestive system?

Mechanical digestion is the physical breaking down of food. For example, the teeth and jaws physically chew food into smaller pieces for further digestion. Chemical digestion occurs when food is altered into different substances more suitable for absorption. Chemical digestion occurs when digestive organs secrete acids and enzymes that break down macronutrients.

Accessory organs—such as the liver and gall bladder—produce secretions (e.g., bile and chemicals) that complete chemical digestion. These organs are considered accessory because food does not directly pass through them as it is being digested.

In a complete digestive system, food is ingested at the mouth, travels through the digestive tract, and excreted at the anus. Vertebrates and complex invertebrates, such as arthropods, contain a complete digestive system. In contrast, an incomplete digestive system contains a digestive cavity with one opening for both ingestion and excretion. This is found among less complex invertebrates, such as cnidarians.

What is the function of villi
in the small intestine?

What is the function of the large
intestine?

What occurs in the process of defecation?

The villi, which are thin structures found within the small intestine, contain multiple folds. These folds increase the surface area of the organ and allow for more efficient nutrient absorption as food passes through the intestine.

The large intestine absorbs water and nutrients remaining in the digestive tract following their exit from the small intestine, then compacts and stores the remaining solid waste and moves it through the rectum for eventual excretion.

Defecation is the final process of digestion, in which solid waste is expelled from the digestive tract. Peristaltic waves in the large intestine move waste to the rectum, where it is held until pressure pushes it out of the anal canal.

What role do kidneys play in osmoregulation?

What path does urine take as it exits the body through the urinary tract?

How does the male urethra function in both the urinary system and reproductive system?

Osmoregulation is the process of balancing the amount of water and salt in bodily fluids, such as blood. Kidneys are responsible for filtering waste from the blood; as blood filters through the kidneys, it maintains osmoregulation through the kidney's excretion of excess water or conservation of water when there is too little of it in the bloodstream.

Urine is created in the kidneys and travels down long, thin ureters to the bladder for storage. The stored urine is eventually released out of the body through the urethra.

In males, urine is excreted out of the body through the urethra as the urethra relaxes and urine stored in the bladder relaxes, which pushes urine out of the body. The male urethra is also the site of ejaculation, during which a mixture of sperm and fluids, called semen, is expelled during intercourse.

Why do gametes—specialized reproductive cells created by sexually reproducing animals—have half of a full set of chromosomes?

Where does oogenesis occur in the female reproductive system?

What are the two main parts of a male sperm cell, and what are their functions?

Sexual reproduction requires one set of genes from each of the two parents. Female gametes (eggs) and male gametes (sperm) are haploid, meaning they have half of a full set of chromosomes. When fertilization occurs, genes from both parents recombine to create genetically distinct offspring.

Oogenesis—the production of eggs—initially begins in the outer layers of the ovaries and matures in the follicles during adolescence.

The head of the sperm cell contains the nucleus as well as an acrosome, which holds enzymes to penetrate a female egg. The tail of the sperm is called a flagellum, which undulates back and forth to create movement.

What are the stages of human embryogenesis?

What are the parts and functions of a neuron, or nerve cell?

What distinguishes the central nervous system and peripheral nervous system from each another?

After fertilization, the newly formed cell, or zygote, divides rapidly to become a blastula during the blastulation process. The cells within the blastula rearrange and start to specialize into distinct germ layers during gastrulation. These germ layers will eventually become specialized tissue and organ systems.

Neurons are comprised of a cell body, dendrite, and an axon. Cell bodies contain the nucleus; dendrites receive impulses from other neurons; and axons transmit impulses across a synapse to another neuron.

The brain and the spinal cord make up the central nervous system and are primarily responsible for processing and integrating external information and coordinating activity throughout the body. The peripheral nervous system is a system of nerves that is responsible for transmitting information back and forth from the various parts of the body to the central nervous system.

What are the components of a reflex arc?

What are the components and function of the brain stem?

Which type of muscle is primarily responsible for all voluntary action in the human body?

A reflex arc is composed of a sensory neuron and a motor neuron. During an involuntary reflex action, the sensory neuron synapses in the spinal cord and activates the motor neuron without first traveling to the brain. This results in a nearly
instantaneous, involuntary motion in response to a stimulus.

The brainstem is comprised of the medulla oblongata, pons, and midbrain. Collectively, these components connect and transmit sensory and motor messages between the brain and the spinal cord. The brainstem also controls many autonomic activities, such as heart rate and breathing.

Skeletal muscles are the only muscles in the body that are controlled consciously. The other types of muscle—cardiac and smooth—are involuntary muscles that control autonomic movement within organ systems.

How do skeletal muscles move?

What is the difference between
fast-twitch fibers and slow-twitch fibers?

How does the cardiac muscle tissue
control contractions of the heart?

Skeletal muscles are typically attached to two bones across a joint. They are anchored by tendons, or dense bands of connective tissue. When muscles contract, they pull on the tendons and move them closer to one another to create skeletal movement.

Type I, or slow-twitch, muscle fibers are fibers that derive energy from aerobic respiration in order to make slow, repeated movements over long periods of time. Type II, or fast-twitch, muscle fibers derive energy from anaerobic respiration in order to produce fast movements for a short period of time.

Cardiac muscle tissue contains specialized cells, called pacemaker cells, which produce electrical charges that stimulate a heartbeat by continuously polarizing and depolarizing it, causing a chain reaction that moves electricity from cell to cell.

What role does bone marrow play in
blood production?

How are tendons, joints, and ligaments
connected and interrelated?

What are the major bones of the
axial skeleton?

Red bone marrow found in some of the human body's bones is the site of blood cell production, or hematopoiesis. The hematopoietic stem cells produced in this marrow create white blood cells, red blood cells, and platelets.

Ligaments, which are bands of flexible tissue, connect two bones together to form a joint. Tendons are flexible tissue bands that attach muscle to two bones that form a joint. Muscles contract to move the bones that are part of the joint, and ligaments protect the bones and joint through this movement.

The axial skeleton protects the vital organs at the center of the human body. It is composed of the skull, which includes cranial, facial, and associated bones; the thorax, which includes the sternum and ribs; and the bones associated with the vertebral column.

What minerals are stored in the
human skeletal system?

What are the functions of the
endocrine system?

What differentiates the posterior pituitary
gland from the anterior pituitary gland?

The bones found in the human skeletal system are a major storage center for calcium and phosphorus and account for the vast majority of these minerals in the body. Magnesium and fluoride are also found in the bones.

The endocrine system secretes hormones into the body to regulate and control major bodily functions, such as metabolism and growth, and respond to stimuli in order to maintain homeostasis.

The posterior pituitary gland, located in the back, receives then transmits hormones produced by the hypothalamus. The anterior pituitary gland, located in the front, produces and releases its own hormones.

How do hormones transmit
chemical messages?

What role does the hypothalamus
play in homeostasis?

Why are physical barriers, such as cilia,
mucus, and saliva, considered nonspecific
defenses of the immune system?

After hormones are secreted and released into the blood-stream, they bind to receptor molecules extending from target cells. Then, the hormones alter the cell's production of proteins, enzymes, and other structures to stimulate the intended change.

The hypothalamus is the portion of the brain that serves as the main link to the endocrine system. It maintains homeo-stasis by regulating the release and inhibition of hormones throughout the body.

Nonspecific defenses are the immune system's way of targeting any pathogen that could potentially pose a threat to the body's well-being. Cilia, mucus, and saliva do not target a specific pathogen; instead, they form a barrier between any foreign object and the body.

What is the difference between the
adaptive immune system
and the innate immune system?

How do helper *T*-cells coordinate
immune responses to pathogens?

What occurs during the process
of phagocytosis?

The innate immune system uses nonspecific defenses to prevent foreign matter from entering the body and attacking any foreign cell that does enter the body. In the adaptive immune system, there is an immune response that recognizes and responds to pathogens that enter the body based on their specific properties.

Helper *T*-cells are a type of lymphocyte that seek out and bind to specific antigens. Once they are bound to the antigen, they stimulate one of two responses: a cell-mediated response or an antibody-mediated response.

During phagocytosis, the phagocyte cell adheres to the foreign or invading particle. The particle is then engulfed within a vacuole, or phagosome, and is digested by enzymes carried by lysosomes within the cell.

What are the different layers of the
dermis, and what are their functions?

Why do sudoriferous glands in the
dermis produce sweat?

What role does the integumentary system
play in vitamin *D* synthesis?

There are two distinct dermis layers of the skin: the papillary and the reticular. The papillary layer delivers blood and nutrients to the epidermis and contains nerve cells to receive messages from outer stimuli. The reticular layer is made of collagen and elastin fibers, which give skin its strength and elasticity.

Sudoriferous glands produce sweat, which travels to the skin and evaporates in order to lower the body's temperature. Waste materials are also excreted through sweat as a way to reduce their presence inside the body.

Cells within the epidermis produce vitamin *D* in response to exposure to ultraviolet light, which is received from sunlight. The skin also functions to store vitamin *D*.

What is the function of keratinization?

What occurs during a negative feedback loop in the human body?

How do the endocrine, cardiovascular, and lymphatic systems work together to fight disease?

Keratinization is the hardening process of the keratin protein in skin, hair, and nail cells. These hardened cells help protect the skin, hair, and nails from damage and foreign particles.

Feedback loops play a major role in maintaining homeostasis. During a negative feedback loop, which is the most common loop, the body responds to an external change by eliciting a response to counteract the change and return the body to homeostasis.

White blood cells are produced in response to chemical stimuli sent to the target organ by the endocrine system. They are transported to the site of infection or site of a foreign invader via the vessels of the cardiovascular and lymphatic systems.

What types of substances are transported by the lymphatic system?

What is the function of lymphatic capillaries?

The lymphatic system transports many different types of interstitial fluid, including water, waste materials, and hormones. It delivers white blood cells to sites of damage or infection and fatty acids from the digestive system to the cardiovascular system.

Lymphatic capillaries are small vessels of the lymphatic system that absorb excess fluids from tissues throughout the body in order to maintain a balanced fluid level in the body.

2

BIOLOGY

enzyme

eukaryote

An enzyme is a protein produced by the cells of living organisms. It functions as a catalyst, accelerating or instigating specific
biochemical reactions within an organism.

Eukaryotic cells are cells that contain membrane-bound organelles, including a true nucleus enclosed by a nuclear envelope and a mitochondrion that acts as an energy-producing powerhouse of the cell.

cytokinesis

nucleotide

histone

Cytokinesis is the division of a parent cell's cytoplasm that occurs after mitosis is complete.

Nucleotides are molecules that serve as the building blocks of nucleic acids (DNA and RNA). They are comprised of a phosphate group, a five-carbon sugar, and a nitrogenous base.

Histones are proteins that are found in chromatin and function as spools around which DNA strands can wrap themselves. They organize DNA strands into structures known as nucleosomes.

rough endoplasmic reticulum

phospholipid bilayer

chromosome

the organelle within the cells of eukaryotes that produces proteins via ribosomes attached to its outer layer

the polar membrane that creates a barrier around cells by providing a hydrophobic interior layer and a hydrophilic exterior layer

the strand-like structure of genetic material that carries the genetic information of the cell within the nucleus

messenger RNA (mRNA)

allele

plasmid

the group of RNA molecules that delivers information transcribed from DNA to ribosomes for protein synthesis

An allele is one version of a pair of genes that is found on the same spot on a chromosome and controls the same trait in an organism. Individuals inherit one allele from each parent.

Plasmids are DNA-containing molecules that are separate from chromosomal DNA and replicate independently. They are typically small, circular, form in the cytoplasm of prokaryotes, and commonly used in genetic engineering techniques.

recessive

sexual selection

cell

a descriptive term for an allele or gene whose phenotype is masked by a more dominant allele or gene in an organism; a trait that an organism does not express; the organism carries the phenotype's genetic information and passes it on to offspring

the form of mating during which organisms choose their mates based on advantageous or desirable traits

the simplest level of biological organization within an organism

deoxyribose

germline mutation

lysosome

Deoxyribose is the sugar found in DNA. It has one less oxygen atom than its counterpart in RNA— ribose—and is therefore more stable in structure.

A germline mutation is an inherited mutation that arises from alterations made to the sperm and egg cells; it is transmitted to offspring.

a membrane-bound organelle created by the Golgi apparatus and used to break down food material found in animal cells that contain enzymes

trait

F1 generation

allele frequency

In genetics, a trait is a characteristic or feature expressed in an organism. The type of trait expressed in an organism is called a phenotype and is determined by the DNA found in the genetic material for that particular trait.

The F1 generation is also called the first filial generation and is the first generation of offspring produced in a genetic cross experiment. Since the parents, or P generation, are selected for being homozygous for a particular trait, the offspring will be heterozygous for the selected trait.

Allele frequency is the rate of occurrence of a specific allele within the gene pool of a population. Allele frequency is determined by the use of the Hardy-Weinberg equation.

interphase

sex-linked traits

trisomy

During the interphase stage of the cell cycle, the cell performs its regular functions to sustain life— such as cellular respiration—while also doubling in size and duplicating its DNA in preparation for division.

genetically linked traits that are located on either the X or Y chromosome of an individual organism

a form of nondisjunction that results in an extra chromosome being added to a cell during meiosis, leading to genetic disorders such as Down syndrome

artificial selection

adaptation

What are the four major biological macromolecules?

the mechanism of evolution that occurs when humans intentionally breed organisms with similar advantageous traits

an inherited trait that becomes common across populations or species due to natural selection and helps an organism become better fitted to its environment

Carbohydrates, lipids, proteins, and nucleic acids are the four major biological macromolecules. Carbohydrates provide energy; lipids store energy and provide structure to cells; proteins perform chemical reactions; and nucleic acids provide genetic information for cells.

Why is water necessary for cells to perform life functions?

Why are cell membranes composed of lipids?

Why are bacteria considered prokaryotic cells?

Water accounts for approximately two thirds of the material of every cell. All water molecules are comprised of two hydrogen atoms bonded to one oxygen atom. Water forms essential bonds with carbon, which is the element necessary for life and the site of all chemical reactions within a cell.

Lipids are generally composed of fatty acids and glycerol. Their chemical arrangement prevents them from mixing with water. This allows the lipids within the cell membrane to maintain and regulate the barrier between water within the cell and water outside the cell.

Bacteria cells, along with archaea cells, are single-celled organisms that do not contain a true nucleus or membrane-bound organelles. The term *prokaryotic* is derived from Greek terminology that means *before nucleus*.

Which organelles differentiate plant cells from animal cells?

Why do cells in multicellular organisms divide?

What are the rules of base pairing in DNA?

Plant cells contain organelles that are not found in animal cells: chloroplasts, which are required for photosynthesis; cell walls, which provide plant cells with a rigid structure; and vacuoles, which are fluid-filled sacs in the cytoplasm that store nutrients and waste.

Cell division occurs in multicellular, eukaryotic organisms in order to grow the organism's size, specialize in specific functions during the organism's development, and repair aged and damaged cells.

DNA has four types of nitrogen bases: adenine (A), thymine (T), guanine (G), and cytosine (C). Adenine pairs with thymine, while guanine pairs with cytosine.

What is the function of RNA?

What are the primary physical differences between DNA and RNA?

What is the most common source of gene mutation in DNA?

Ribonucleic acid (RNA) molecules are responsible for synthesizing protein and transmitting genetic information. There are three major types of RNA: mRNA—messenger RNA that carries information from DNA; rRNA—ribosomal RNA that forms ribosomes for protein synthesis; and tRNA—transfer RNA that brings mRNA to the ribosomes.

DNA and RNA are nucleic acids that perform different functions within the cell. DNA is double stranded, while RNA is single stranded. DNA contains deoxyribose—a sugar—and has four bases: adenine, thymine, guanine, and cytosine. RNA contains ribose instead of deoxyribose, and has uracil as a base instead of thymine.

The majority of gene mutation occurs when DNA is copied incorrectly during the replication process. A single change to one base in a nucleotide can have a dramatic impact on the organism and cause a disease or disorder.

What is the difference between
genotypes and phenotypes?

Why do different combinations of alleles
in an organism's genotype result in
different phenotypes?

What are the laws of heredity that form
the basis of Mendelian genetics?

A genotype is the combination of genes inherited from parents; a phenotype is the observable trait that is expressed in an organism.

If an organism inherits identical alleles for a genotype from each parent, the genotype is considered homozygous, and the organism will express the same trait. If an organism inherits different types of alleles from each parent, then the genotype is considered heterozygous, in which case the dominant allele will be expressed while the recessive allele will not.

Mendelian genetics are founded upon three laws: the laws of segregation, independent assortment, and dominance. The law of segregation is based on the principle that genes separate into distinct alleles during meiosis. According to the law of independent assortment, these genes separate and recombine independently of one another, with every combination of alleles having equal chances to occur. The law of dominance states that offspring will express the dominant allele.

What is the purpose of dihybrid crosses?

What do the squares and circles represent in a pedigree chart? What do filled and unfilled shapes represent?

How are homozygous and heterogeneous genes represented in a Punnett square?

Dihybrid crosses are performed in order to isolate two different inherited traits from a set of parents to study how they are inherited and expressed through multiple generations of offspring. This helps determine whether or not any relationship exists between the two sets of alleles.

In a pedigree chart, males are represented by squares and females are represented by circles. Symbols that are fully filled in represent family members who are homozygous for a dominant trait; symbols that are partially filled in represent family members who are heterozygous for a dominant trait; symbols that are not filled in represent family members who are homozygous for a recessive trait.

Homozygous genes, which are genes that contain identical alleles from each parent, are referred to by two capital letters if the trait is dominant and by two lowercase letters if the trait is recessive. To contrast, heterozygous genes are referred to by a capital letter—representing the dominant allele—and a lowercase letter, which represents the recessive allele.

What distinguishes Mendelian genetics from non-Mendelian genetics?

What occurs during the process of recombination?

Why are recessive *X*-linked genetic traits expressed primarily in males but not females?

Mendel's laws of heredity apply to traits that are controlled by a single gene that has two potential alleles: one dominant and one recessive. Not all traits are controlled by these same patterns. Non-Mendelian genetics refers to patterns that are studied and observed in traits that do not have dominant/recessive allele relationships, traits that have more than two possible alleles, and traits that are controlled by multiple genes.

Recombination (crossing over) occurs during prophase I of meiosis. As duplicated chromosomes separate into chromatids, the chromatids intertwine and exchange alleles in random patterns. The resultant chromosome therefore carries the same genes but has a combination of both paternal and maternal alleles.

Females carry two X chromosomes, while males carry an X chromosome and a Y chromosome. If a female inherits a recessive X-linked allele, the phenotype has a greater chance of being masked by a dominant X-linked allele. Males inherit only one X-linked allele, so the allele will be expressed regardless of whether it is the dominant or recessive allele.

Why are height and weight considered examples of traits that display continuous variation?

How is extranuclear DNA passed on from parent to offspring?

How do chromosomal abnormalities increase genetic diversity and drive evolution among a population of organisms?

Unlike eye color—a trait for which there is not a set number of varieties—height and weight are traits that exist along a continuum.

Some organelles, including chloroplasts and mitochondria, contain DNA that does not replicate during gamete formation because it is not located within the nucleus. DNA in these organelles is duplicated from the maternal cell when two gametes fertilize, and the offspring inherits extranuclear DNA exclusively from the mother.

Some chromosomal abnormalities introduce new genes and changes to phenotypes that are expressed among a population of organisms. In sexually reproducing eukaryotes, these phenotypes can give organisms an ecological advantage and are more likely to be selected for and passed on in a population.

How do evolutionary mechanisms lead to change in populations of sexually reproducing organisms?

How do ecological relationships lead to coevolution of two or more species?

Why do homologous structures in living organisms indicate evidence of evolutionary relationships?

Evolutionary mechanisms, such as natural selection, alter the variation of genetic information and allele frequency within the population. These changes alter the reproductive patterns of a population; certain traits survive while others do not. This results in a gradual change to the population of organisms over time.

During coevolution, two species with a close ecological relationship impact the evolution of the other species, and vice versa. This is seen among predator-prey relationships as one species evolves to catch or evade the other; among competitive species as they differentiate to occupy different niches; and among mutualistic species, which evolve mutually beneficial mechanisms in response to one another.

Homology of structural features between two species indicates that the species shared a common ancestor at some point in its evolutionary history. This is an example of one piece of evidence of evolutionary relationships between two species.

3

CHEMISTRY

physical property

elements

A physical property is a property, like color, that can be observed without changing the identity of the substance.

Elements are substances made up of only one type of particle. These individual particles can be atoms, as in the case of neon gas, or molecules, as is the case with oxygen gas, which is made up of O_2 molecules.

mixture

specific heat

mass number

A mixture is matter composed of two or more substances.

The specific heat of a substance is the amount of heat energy necessary to change the temperature of one gram of the substance by one degree Celsius. Substances have characteristic specific heats, and therefore the specific heat of a substance can be used to identify the substance.

The mass number is the sum of the number of protons and neutrons in the nucleus of an atom.

isotopes

cation

covalent bonds

Isotopes are atoms of the same element with a different number of neutrons and therefore different mass numbers.

A cation is a positively charged ion. It is formed by removing electrons from the neutral atom. In so doing, a more stable electron configuration is achieved.

Covalent bonds are bonds between two atoms which involve the sharing of electrons.

chemical property

law of conservation of mass

combustion reaction

A chemical property describes what happens to a substance when it undergoes a chemical reaction. In this chemical reaction, the substance is changed into a new, different substance.

The law of conservation of mass states that matter cannot be created or destroyed in a chemical reaction. In other words, the total mass of the products of a reaction must equal the total mass of the reactants.

A combustion reaction is the reaction of a substance with oxygen. The most common combustion reactions involve reacting an organic compound—a carbon-based compound—with oxygen, producing CO_2 and H_2O.

endothermic reaction

valance electrons

synthesis reaction

In an endothermic reaction, heat energy is absorbed. The heat energy can be listed as a reactant in the balanced equation.

Valence electrons are the electrons in the outermost occupied energy level in an atom.

In a synthesis reaction, two or more substances are combined to form a single substance.

phase transition

anion

decomposition reaction

A phase transition refers to a substance undergoing a change in its physical state. When a substance goes from a solid to a liquid state, a phase change, it has melted. When a substance goes from a liquid to a gas state, a phase change, it has boiled.

An anion is a negatively charged ion formed by adding electrons to the neutral atom. In so doing, a more stable electron configuration is achieved.

A decomposition reaction involves the breakdown of a single substance into two or more simpler substances.

single displacement reaction

surface tension

sublimation

In a single displacement reaction, an element reacts with a compound. The single element replaces an element in the compound.

Surface tension refers to a force that acts on the surface of a liquid and makes its surface area as small as possible. For example, a given volume of a liquid will have the smallest surface area when it has a spherical shape. This accounts for the shape of drops of rain.

Sublimation is the process in which a substance transforms directly from the solid state to the gaseous state.

products

condensation

boiling point

The products in a chemical reaction are the substances that are formed. They appear on the right in a chemical equation.

Condensation is the phase change in which a gas becomes a liquid. Water vapor in the air often condenses on colder surfaces. Dew is an example.

The boiling point of a liquid is the temperature at which the vapor pressure of the liquid equals the external pressure. When these two pressures are equal, little bubbles can form in the liquid, and boiling occurs.

triple point

neutrons

neutralization reaction

On a phase diagram, the triple point represents the temperature and pressure conditions at which all three phases of a substance exist and are in equilibrium.

A neutron is one of the three types of subatomic particles that make up atoms. Neutrons have no charge and are located in the nucleus. An atom of an element must have a certain number of protons, but its number of neutrons can vary.

A neutralization reaction is the reaction of an Arrhenius acid with an Arrhenius base that produces a salt and water.

electron

halogens

transition metals

An electron is one of the three types of subatomic particles that make up atoms. They are minuscule, negatively charged particles located in regions around the nucleus called energy levels. In a neutral atom the number of electrons equals the number of protons.

The halogens are the elements of Group VII. These elements are the most reactive of the nonmetals, readily gaining one electron to form −1 ions.

The transition metals are the thirty elements in the center of the periodic table, which are involved with filling sets of d-orbitals. The transition metals are less reactive than the elements of Groups I and II. They are good conductors of heat and electricity.

phase diagram

reactants

proton

A phase diagram is the graph of the physical states of a substance that exist at different temperature and pressure conditions.

The reactants in a chemical reaction are the initial substances. They appear on the left in a chemical equation.

A proton is one of the three types of subatomic particles that make up atoms. Protons are positively charged and located in the nucleus of the atom. The number of protons in a nucleus determines the element. In chemical reactions, the number of protons in a nucleus never changes.

Is melting considered a chemical or physical change?

How are the electron configurations of the elements in a group on the periodic table alike?

What are the two types of covalent bonds and how do they differ?

Melting is a physical change since the particles remain the same. They are simply given energy which allows the particles to move about and enter the liquid phase.

All the elements in a group have the same number of valence electrons.

The two types of covalent bonds are polar covalent bonds and nonpolar covalent bonds. In nonpolar covalent bonds, the two atoms share the electrons evenly. There is no separation of charge; no electrical poles are formed. Hence, they are called *nonpolar* covalent bonds. In polar covalent bonds, the two atoms share the electrons unevenly. The electrons are pulled closer to one of the atoms and electrical poles develop. This accounts for the name *polar* covalent bonds.

What type of reaction is $AgNO_3(aq)$ + $NaCl(aq) \rightarrow AgCl(s) + NaNO_3(aq)$?

What are the five common types of chemical reactions?

How many electrons are shared by two atoms joined by a triple covalent bond?

a double displacement reaction

combustion reactions, synthesis reactions, decomposition reactions, single displacement reactions, and double displacement reactions.

six (three pairs)

What are covalent compounds?

In which physical state do the particles have the greatest freedom of movement?

What are the physical properties of water, and how are they affected by its polarity?

Covalent compounds usually involve two or more nonmetals whose electronegativities are similar. The atoms in the molecules in covalent compounds share electrons.

The gaseous state allows particles greatest freedom of movement. In a solid state, the individual particles are close together and held in position. In a liquid state, particles can move freely over one another allowing liquids to flow. In a gaseous state, the particles have been pulled apart; they are separated by empty space.

Water has higher melting and boiling points than expected because of the increased interaction between the polar water molecules. Water is an excellent solvent for dissolving salts: the charged ions making up the salt can interact with the polar water molecules.

What are the properties of
ionic compounds?

Name the three major physical states
of matter.

Identify three physical properties
of matter.

The attractive forces between the oppositely charged ions in ionic compounds are strong. Therefore ionic compounds will have high melting and boiling points. Liquid ionic compounds dissolved in aqueous solutions will conduct electricity. Most ionic compounds are hard and brittle as solids.

solid, liquid, gas

Possible answers include: melting point, boiling point, color, and density.

Explain how the atoms of an element can have different mass numbers.

What particles make up the nucleus of an atom?

What property of an atom determines its element?

Despite sharing the same number of protons, the atoms of an element can have different mass numbers because they can have a different number of neutrons.

protons and neutrons

The quantity that determines the identity of an atom is the number of protons in the nucleus of the atom. The number of protons in the nucleus of every atom of an element is called the atomic number of the element. Atomic numbers are given on a periodic table.

What are the two types of pure
substances, those made up of
only one kind of particle?

What type of a reaction is
$C_3H_8 + 5O_2 \rightarrow 3CO_2 + 4H_2O$?

How does the density of ice compare to
the density of water?

elements and compounds

A combustion reaction

Ice is less dense than water because water molecules crystal-ize to form a very open structure with a lot of empty space. Hence ice has a lower density; for instance, ice cubes float in water.

4

MATHEMATICS

How is a proportion solved?

Describe the process for
dividing fractions.

cross-multiply

$$\frac{a}{b} = \frac{c}{d} \rightarrow ad = bc$$

To divide fractions, multiply the first fraction by the reciprocal of the second fraction.

$$\frac{a}{b} \div \frac{c}{d} = \frac{a}{b} \times \frac{d}{c} = \frac{ad}{bc}$$

How is a decimal converted to a percent?

Which terms in the expression
$3xy^2 + 6xy - 3y^2 - xy^2$ can be added?

In the following expression, which
operation is performed first?
$4(5 + (6 - 8)^3) + 2$

multiply the decimal by 100

$0.37 \times 100 = 37\%$

$3xy^2$ and $-xy^2$

Only terms with the same variables can be added.

$6 - 8$

According to the order of operations—PEMDAS—operations inside parentheses are performed first. When parentheses are nested, start with the innermost set.

Will an outlier have the biggest effect on the value of the mean, median, or mode?

What units can be used to measure volume?

Describe the process for multiplying fractions.

Outliers affect mean by shifting it away from the median. Outliers do not affect mode.

liters (L), cubic meters (m³), fluid ounces (fl oz), pints (pt), quarts (qt), gallons (gal)

To multiply fractions, multiply across and simplify.
$\frac{a}{b} \times \frac{c}{d} = \frac{ac}{bd}$

Multiplying a negative number by a negative number always results in a _____ number.

What is a mixed number?

What is the distributive property?

positive

a number with a whole number part and a fraction part

The distributive property is used to multiply a single term by two or more terms inside a set of parentheses.

$a(b + c + d) = ab + ac + ad$

How can miles per hour be converted
to feet per second?

What is the formula for the area
of a circle?

What does PEMDAS stand for?

Multiply the original value by the appropriate conversion factors. The original units should cancel, leaving only the new units.

$$\frac{x \text{ miles}}{\text{hour}} \times \frac{5,280 \text{ feet}}{1 \text{ mile}} \times \frac{1 \text{ hour}}{60 \text{ seconds}} = \frac{(x)(5,280) \text{ feet}}{60 \text{ second}}$$

$A = \pi r^2$

The order of operations: parentheses, exponents, multiplication/division, and addition/subtraction.

$x^0 =$

$x^0 = 1$

What is the *y*-intercept of the line
$y = 3x - 2$?

Describe the process for adding and
subtracting fractions.

What is the mode of a data set?

−2

To add or subtract fractions, convert each denominator to the common denominator, add or subtract the numerators, and then simplify the result.

Mode is the number that occurs most often in the set.

What is a bar graph?

Which of the following numbers satisfies
the inequality $0 < x \le 8$?

0, 4, 8, 12

What is the formula for the
circumference of a circle?

A bar graph consists of a series of vertical or horizontal bars that show the frequency of each value or category.

4 and 8

$C = 2\pi r$

How many degrees are there in a triangle?

The average newborn sleeps eighteen hours a day, and children require at least ten hours of sleep until age nine. Adults, however, only require eight hours of sleep a day.

In this scenario, is there a positive correlation or a negative correlation between age and hours of sleep required?

Which number is the largest?
$$\sqrt{25}, \frac{12}{3}, 2^2$$

180°

This scenario describes a negative correlation between age and hours of sleep required: as one variable goes up (age), the other variable goes down (hours of sleep).

$\sqrt{25} = 5$

$\frac{12}{3} = 4$

$2^2 = 4$

$\sqrt{25}$ is the largest number.

How many degrees are in a quadrilateral?

What is the mean of a data set?

Express the phrase "six more than three times *x*" mathematically.

360°

Mean is the average value, or the sum of the values divided by the number of values in the set.

$3x + 6$

What is the formula for finding slope?

What information is shown in a pie chart?

What is the formula for the area
of a rectangle?

$$m = \frac{y_2 - y_1}{x_2 - x_1}$$

Pie charts show the percentages of each element of a set.

$A = lw$

l = length and w = width

What is the area of a square with a
side length of 6 m?

What decimal is equivalent to 45%?

What is $\frac{27}{4}$ as a mixed number?

$A = s^2 = 6^2 = 36 \text{ m}^2$

$45\% = 0.45$

$27 \div 4 = 6$ with a remainder of 3

$\frac{27}{4} = 6\frac{3}{4}$

What is the median of a data set?

In the number 12,408.57, what place is the number 7 in?

Median is the number in the middle of the set.

hundredths

5

READING

main idea

topic

the argument the author makes in a text passage

what a text passage is about

topic sentence

summary sentence

supporting detail

the sentence that introduces the topic of a text passage; often the first sentence in the passage

a sentence that summarizes the main idea and key details of a text passage; often the last sentence in the passage

a statement in a text passage that supports the main idea

fact

opinion

inference

a statement that can be proven true

a personal belief that cannot be substantiated with proof

a conclusion drawn from the information in a text passage and the reader's own knowledge; not explicitly stated in the passage

conclusion

explicit information

implicit information

an educated guess about what happens next given the explicit information in a text passage

information that is directly stated in a text passage

information that can be inferred from a text passage but is not stated outright

signal words

legend

compass

words used to introduce, or "signal," an important piece of
information in a text passage or to explain the relationship
between ideas in a passage

the section of map that explains what the map's symbols
mean

a four- or eight-pointed shape on a map that indicates
direction (north, northeast, east, etc.)

scale

What are the four ways to structure text?

point of view

a line on a map marked to show the relationship between distance on the map and real-life distance

chronological (time), cause and effect, problem/solution, and compare/contrast

the author's position or belief about a subject

tone

mode

connotation

the author's attitude about a subject, usually described with a single word such as *critical* or *optimistic*

the author's purpose for writing a passage; can be expository, persuasive, or narrative

the implied meaning of a word created by context and usage

denotation

figurative language

prefix

the dictionary definition of a word

language used beyond its literal meaning; includes devices like metaphors and hyperbole (exaggeration)

a set of letters added to the beginning of a word to change its meaning

suffix

root word

italics

a set of letters added to the end of the word to change its meaning

a word with no prefix or suffix

tilted font used for titles of works, including books and movies, foreign words, and names of ships

bold text

index

table of contents

dark font used to emphasize words

a list in the back of a book that includes the topics included in the book and the page numbers where they appear

a list at the beginning of a book that shows chapters (and sometimes headings or subheadings) and the page where they begin

primary source

secondary source

tertiary source

a source of information provided by a participant in or witness to an event

a source of information created by someone who did not participate in or witness an event; created after an event has occurred

a list of primary and secondary sources, such as a bibliography or index

Between November 15 and December 21, 1864, Major General William Tecumseh Sherman marched Union troops from the recently captured city of Atlanta to the port of Savannah. The goal was not only to capture the port city and secure Georgia for the Union, but also to destroy the Confederacy's infrastructure and demoralize its people.

Where did General Sherman and his troops begin marching on November 15?

The cisco, a foot-long freshwater fish native to the Great Lakes, had almost died out by the 1950s, but today it thrives. The cisco have an invasive species, quagga mussels, to thank for their return. Quagga mussels depleted nutrients in the lakes, harming other species highly dependent on these nutrients. Cisco, however, thrive in low-nutrient environments. As other species—many invasive—diminished, cisco flourished in their place.

How did quagga mussels prevent the cisco's extinction?

In 1953, doctors surgically removed the hippocampus of patient Henry Molaison in an attempt to stop his frequent seizures. Unexpectedly, he lost the ability to form new memories, leading to the biggest breakthrough in the science of memory. Molaison's long-term memory—of events more than a year before his surgery—was unchanged as was his ability to learn physical skills. From this, scientists learned that different types of memory are handled by different parts of the brain.

Based on the text, which part of the brain probably handles the task of forming new memories?

Atlanta, Georgia; the text says that they marched "from the recently captured city of Atlanta to the port of Savannah."

Quagga mussels depleted nutrients in the Great Lakes, harming species that needed them. Since the cisco thrives in low-nutrient environments, and because it now had fewer species to compete with, this freshwater fish stopped dying out and began to thrive again.

The hippocampus probably handles the task of forming new memories—after doctors removed Molaison's hippocampus, "he lost the ability to form new memories."

Archaeologists have discovered the oldest known specimens of bedbugs in a cave in Oregon where humans once lived. The three species found in the Oregon caves are actually still around today, although they continue to prefer bats. Humans only lived seasonally in the Oregon cave system, which might explain why these insects did not fully transfer to human hosts like bedbugs elsewhere did.

Today, why do the three species of bedbugs prefer bats to humans?

At midnight on Saturday, August 12, 1961, units of the East German army moved into position and began closing the border between East and West Berlin. Destroying streets that ran parallel to the border to make them impassable, they installed ninety-seven miles of barbed wire and fences around West Berlin and another twenty-seven miles along the border between West and East Berlin.

Was the author's main purpose for writing this passage to inform readers or to express an opinion? Explain how you know.

In 1974, scientists uncovered in Africa's Rift Valley a 3.2 million-year-old nonhuman hominid they nicknamed Lucy. And in 2013, researchers found the oldest fossil in the human ancestral line. Before the 2013 discovery, the oldest fossil from the genus Homo—of which *Homo sapiens* is the only remaining species—dated back only 2.3 million years, leaving a 700,000 year gap between Lucy's species and the advent of humans. The new fossil dated back to between 2.75 and 2.8 million years ago, pushing the appearance of humans back 400,000 years.

Name two important differences between Lucy and the fossil discovered in 2013.

The bedbugs probably did not "fully transfer to human hosts" because humans did not live year-round in the caves where the bedbugs lived.

The author's main purpose is to inform readers; no opinions are expressed, only facts.

Lucy was a "nonhuman hominid," and the fossil discovered in 2013 was "in the human ancestral line." Lucy was 3.2 million years old, and the 2013 fossil was about 2.8 million years old—so Lucy was about 400,000 years older.

There are many situations when measuring temperature orally isn't an option. Some people, like agitated patients or fussy babies, won't be able to sit still long enough for an accurate reading. In these situations, it's best to use a thermometer that works much more quickly, such as one that measures temperature in the ear or at the temporal artery.

According to the passage, in what situation is it best to use a thermometer that works quickly?

A study of people who'd lost a high percentage of their body weight (>17%) in a short period of time found that they could not physically maintain their new weight. Scientists measured their resting metabolic rate and found that they'd need to consume only a few hundred calories a day to meet their metabolic needs. Basically, their bodies were in starvation mode and seemed to desperately hang on to each and every calorie.

Why did dieters' bodies go into "starvation mode"?

In recent decades, jazz has been associated with New Orleans and festivals like Mardi Gras, but in the 1920s, jazz was a booming trend whose influence reached into many aspects of American culture. In fact, the years between World War I and the Great Depression were known as the Jazz Age, a term coined by F. Scott Fitzgerald in his famous novel *The Great Gatsby*. Sometimes also called the Roaring Twenties, this period saw major urban centers experiencing new economic, cultural, and artistic vitality.

Who first called the 1920s "the Jazz Age"?

When a patient cannot "sit still long enough for an accurate reading"; two examples of such a patient are an agitated person or a fussy baby.

Dieters' bodies went into "starvation mode" because they had "lost a high percentage of their body weight (>17%) in a short period of time." According to the passage, when someone loses a lot of weight in a short period of time, the body feels like it is starving and "desperately [hangs] on to each and every calorie."

Writer F. Scott Fitzgerald coined this term in his novel *The Great Gatsby*.

The most important part of brewing coffee is using the right water. Choose a water that you think has a nice, neutral flavor. Anything with too many minerals or contaminants will change the flavor of the coffee, and water with too few minerals won't do a good job of extracting the flavor from the coffee beans. Water should be heated to between 195 and 205 degrees Fahrenheit. Boiling water (212 degrees Fahrenheit) will burn the beans and give your coffee a scorched flavor.

What is the author's main purpose for writing this passage? How can you tell?

Once your coffee beans are ground and the water has reached the perfect temperature, you're ready to brew. A French press (which we recommend), allows you to control brewing time and provide a thorough brew. Pour the grounds into the press, then pour the hot water over the grounds and let it steep. The brew shouldn't require more than 5 minutes, although those of you who like your coffee a bit harsher can leave it longer. Finally, use the plunger to remove the grounds and pour.

What should you do after pouring the coffee grounds into the press?

Although it's a common disease, the flu is not actually highly infectious, meaning it's relatively difficult to contract. The flu can only be transmitted when individuals come into direct contact with bodily fluids of people infected with the flu or when they are exposed to expelled aerosol particles (which result from coughing and sneezing).

Which would be more likely to give you the flu: shaking hands with an infected person or sharing a drinking glass with that person? Explain how this can be inferred from the passage.

The author's main purpose is to teach readers how to make good coffee. The author provides detailed instructions on how to do this.

After "pour[ing] the grounds into the press," you should "pour the hot water over the grounds and let it steep."

Sharing a drinking glass with an infected person would be more likely to give you the flu. Sharing a glass would probably cause you to "come into direct contact with" the infected person's saliva, a bodily fluid. (If the person had just sneezed or coughed into her hands, shaking hands with her could give you the flu, too, but then you would have to lick your fingers to transmit the virus to your body.)

One of the reasons the flu has historically been so deadly is the amount of time between when people become infectious and when they develop symptoms. Viral shedding—the process by which the body releases viruses that have been successfully reproducing during the infection—takes place two days after infection, while symptoms do not usually develop until the third day of infection. Thus, infected individuals have at least twenty-four hours in which they may unknowingly infect others.

According to the passage, what happens after infection occurs but before flu symptoms develop?

In the 1950s, scientists learned that different types of memory are handled by different parts of the brain, with the hippocampus responsible for *episodic memory*, the short-term recall of events. Researchers have since discovered that some memories are then channeled to the cortex, the outer layers of the brain that handle higher functions, where they are gradually integrated with related information to build lasting knowledge about our world.

Where is the brain's cortex located?

It seemed to Julia as if the other drivers on the road felt as sluggish and surly as she did—it took her an extra fifteen minutes to get to work. And when she arrived, all the parking spots were full. By the time she'd finally found a spot in the overflow lot, she was thirty minutes late for work. She'd hoped her boss would be too busy to notice, but he'd already put a pile of paperwork on her desk with a note that simply said "Rewrite."

How does Julia know that her boss noticed that she is late for work?

Viral shedding occurs two days after infection and one day before flu symptoms develop.

The cortex is the brain's "outer layers."

He has already put a pile of paperwork on her desk, so he must have noticed that she was not there on time.

The energy needs of patients can vary widely. Generally, energy needs are directly related to a person's weight and inversely related to age; it's also generally true that men require more calories than women. Thus, a thirty-five-year-old woman who weighs 135 pounds will require around 1800 calories a day, while an older woman would require fewer, and a heavier woman would require more. A man of the same age and weight would require 2000 calories a day.

If a sixty-year-old woman who weighs 135 pounds eats 1,800 or more calories a day, what will probably happen?

Food historians believe that popcorn is one of the earliest uses of cultivated corn. In 1948, Herbert Dick and Earle Smith discovered old popcorn dating back 4000 years in the New Mexico Bat Cave. For the Aztec Indians who called the caves home, popcorn (or momochitl) played an important role in society, both as a food staple and in ceremonies. The Aztecs cooked popcorn by heating sand in a fire; when it was heated, kernels were added and would pop when exposed to the heat of the sand.

What did the Aztecs do after heating sand in a fire?

The American love affair with popcorn began in 1912, when popcorn was first sold in theaters. The popcorn industry flourished during the Great Depression when it was advertised as a wholesome and economical food. Selling for five to ten cents a bag, it was a luxury that the downtrodden could afford. With the introduction of mobile popcorn machines at the World's Columbian Exposition, popcorn moved from the theater into fairs and parks.

Use context clues to define the word *downtrodden*.

She will probably gain weight. The passage says that "an older woman [who weighs 135 pounds] would require fewer [calories per day than 1,800]."

They added corn kernels to the heated sand; this caused the kernels to pop, forming popcorn.

During the Great Depression, many people lost their jobs, so they were very poor. By "the downtrodden," the author must mean poor people, people who were beaten down—demoralized—by hard economic times.

Credit scores, which range from 300 to 850, are a single value that summarizes an individual's credit history. Pay your bills late? Your credit score will be lower than someone who gets that electric bill filed on the first of every month. Just paid off your massive student loans? You can expect your credit score to shoot up. The companies that compile credit scores actually keep track of all the loans, credit cards, and bill payments in your name.

What is the highest possible credit score?

Having no credit score can often be just as bad as having a low one. Lenders want to know that you have a history of borrowing money and paying it back on time. After all, if you've never taken out a loan, how can a bank know that you'll pay back its money? So, having nothing on your credit report can result in low credit limits and high interest rates.

What is this passage's main idea?

If you have ever been cut off in the middle of bad city traffic, you may have immediately assumed that the offender was inconsiderate or incompetent. While possible, it may be equally likely that the person is dealing with an emergency situation or that they simply did not see you. According to psychologist Eliot Aronson, this tendency to attribute behaviors, especially negative behaviors, to disposition is risky and can ultimately be detrimental to us by harming our own sense of social obligation and goodwill.

Use context clues to define the word *detrimental*.

The highest possible credit score is 850; the passage says that "credit scores . . . range from 300 to 850."

The main idea is expressed in the first sentence: "Having no credit score can often be just as bad as having a low one." The other sentences in the passage provide details that support this idea.

The author says that attributing negative behaviors to disposition is "detrimental" and leads to "harming our own sense of social obligation and goodwill," implying that *detrimental* means "to cause harm."

At the beginning of Philip Zimbardo's famous prison experiment, the participants, all healthy, stable, intelligent male Stanford University students, were classified as either guards or prisoners and told they would be acting their parts in a simulated prison environment for two weeks. However, after just six days, Zimbardo had to terminate the experiment because of the extreme behaviors he was witnessing in both groups: prisoners had become entirely submissive to and resentful of the guards, while the guards had become cruel and unrelenting in their treatment of the prisoners.

How did the experiment cause participants to act?

Martin Seligman's 2011 book is titled *Flourish: A Visionary New Understanding of Happiness and Well-being.* The author's well-being theory addresses not only life satisfaction but also the extent to which one flourishes in his or her life. According to this theory, an individual's well-being is determined by—in addition to subjective experiences like positive emotions, engagement, and meaning—external factors like constructive relationships and personal achievement.

According to Seligman, which "external factors" help an individual to flourish?

Though positive psychology is a relatively young field within the social sciences, it has already made great strides in attracting attention from researchers and practitioners in the field. Further, it has already begun to gain popular attention, proving that it is on its way to meeting the goal that Dr. Seligman initially set out to accomplish—to have a positive impact on the lives of everyday people who might otherwise have no motivation to seek therapy.

What does the author mean by "a relatively young field"?

The ones playing prisoners became "entirely submissive to and resentful of the guards," while the ones playing guards became "cruel and unrelenting in their treatment of the prisoners."

"External factors like constructive relationships and personal achievement" help an individual to flourish.

The author means that positive psychology is a field that developed recently.

According to veterinarian Debbie Grant, three myths are especially detrimental to the cause of animal pain management. The first of these is the myth that animals do not feel pain at all or that they feel it less intensely than humans; in fact, according to Grant, the biological mechanisms by which we experience pain are the very same mechanisms by which animals experience pain. Even the emotional reaction to a painful experience (like being afraid to return to the dentist after an unpleasant visit) is mirrored in animals.

Does this passage express facts or opinions?

Animals do not necessarily tolerate pain any better than humans do, though they may handle their pain differently. Dr. Debbie Grant emphasizes that veterinarians must be aware that a lack of obvious signs does not necessarily suggest that pain is not present: in fact, many animals, especially those that are prey animals in the wild, are likely to conceal their pain out of an instinct to hide weaknesses that may make them easy targets for predators.

According to the passage, why are prey animals likely to conceal their pain?

In 2014, researchers of veterinary medicine at the University of Perugia in Italy completed a review of the diagnostic tools and strategies available to today's practitioners and found a number of them to be effective. Presumptive diagnosis, the first of these strategies, involves making a prediction about the animal's pain based on the observable damage to the body or body part. As with human pain, greater damage or disfigurement likely suggests more significant pain.

Where and when did veterinary researchers study the diagnostic tools and strategies available to today's veterinarians?

The passage expresses Dr. Debbie Grant's opinions on myths that "are especially detrimental to the cause of animal pain management."

They conceal their pain because they have "an instinct to hide weaknesses that may make them easy targets for predators."

In 2014 at the University of Perugia in Italy.

Water is found in primitive bodies like comets and asteroids, and dwarf planets like Ceres. The atmospheres and interiors of the four giant planets—Jupiter, Saturn, Uranus and Neptune—are thought to contain enormous quantities of the wet stuff, and their moons and rings have substantial water ice.

Perhaps the most surprising water worlds are the five icy moons of Jupiter and Saturn that show strong evidence of oceans beneath their surfaces: Ganymede, Europa and Callisto at Jupiter, and Enceladus and Titan at Saturn.

How many of Saturn's moons show evidence of water beneath their surfaces?

Two: Enceladus and Titan

6

ENGLISH AND LANGUAGE USAGE

noun

pronoun

a word that names a person, place, or thing

a word (such as *I*, *me*, *he*, *she*, *him*, *her*, *you*, *it*, *we*, *us*, *them*, or *they*) that is used in place of a noun

subject pronoun

verb

predicate

a pronoun (such as *I*, *he*, *she*, *you*, *it*, *we*, or *they*) that is used as the subject of a sentence

a word that forms the main part of a sentence's predicate and describes an action, state of being, or event

the part of a sentence that includes a verb and tells what the sentence's subject is or does

adjective

adverb

conjunction

a word that modifies (provides detailed information about) a noun or pronoun

a word that modifies (provides detailed information about) a verb, adjective, or adverb

a word that joins words, phrases, or clauses

coordinating conjunction

subordinating conjunction

interjection

a conjunction (such as *and, or, but, so, yet,* or *nor*) that connects words, phrases, or clauses of equal value

a conjunction (such as *although, because, as, while, until, whether, since, after, when, before,* or *if*) that begins a subordinate (dependent) clause and connects it to a main (independent) clause

a part of speech that reveals a writer's or speaker's emotions and sometimes interrupts the flow of conversation; examples: *oh, wow, wait, hey, ouch*); often followed by an exclamation point

phrase

preposition

simple sentence

a small group of words that stand together as a unit and suggest a certain image or idea; examples: *bicycling down a shady country road* or *my oldest cat*

a word that shows the relationship between two other nearby words; examples: *on*, *by*, *to*, *from*, *under*, *over*, *with*, or *beside*

a sentence that includes only one clause (Example: *I always brush my teeth before I go to bed.*)

compound sentence

complex sentence

independent clause

a sentence made up of two or more simple sentences joined by a conjunction and/or an appropriate punctuation mark; examples: *I always brush my teeth before I go to bed, and I also brush them after breakfast. I always brush my teeth before I go to bed; I also brush them after breakfast.*

a sentence made up of one independent (main) clause and one or more dependent (subordinate) clauses (Example: *While I don't want to miss my bus, I can stay a few minutes longer.*)

a clause that forms a simple sentence or can be combined with one or more dependent (subordinate) clauses to form a complex sentence (Example: *I can stay a few minutes longer.*)

dependent clause

semicolon

subject

a clause that begins with a subordinating conjunction (such as *although*, *while*, *since*, or *because*) and can be combined with an independent (main) clause to form a complex sentence (Example: *Although I don't want to miss my bus …*)

a punctuation mark (;) that indicates a medium-length pause between two independent clauses in a compound sentence (Example: *I need to buy milk at the store; I should try to remember what else I need.*)

a word or phrase that tells who or what a sentence is about; may include adjectives and/or adjective phrases (Example: *That dog over there was born in Thailand.*)

FIND THE ERROR:

Not every nation has a President as its leader; some have prime ministers, some have kings or queens, and others have military dictators.

FIND THE ERROR:

In our club, everyone who attends the meetings stay afterward to help clean up.

FIND THE ERROR:

First we will fly to Copenhagen, a port city in Denmark and then we will board a ship and sail to several different Baltic nations.

In this sentence, *president* is a common noun (a noun that names more than one person), so it should not be capitalized.

The plural verb *stay* does not agree with its singular subject, *everyone*. *Stay* should be replaced with *stays*.

This compound sentence needs a comma inserted after *Denmark* and before the conjunction *and*.

FIND THE ERROR:

It is Ana's birthday next Wednesday, we're planning a family celebration for the following weekend.

FIND THE ERROR:

The two older people are Shelby's great-grandparents standing over there.

FIND THE ERROR:

Which State in the United States is larger, Alaska or Texas?

This is an incorrectly constructed sentence (a comma splice). It needs a conjunction such as *so* or *and* following the comma and before the word *we're*.

The adjective phrase "standing over there" is misplaced in the sentence. It should be moved to follow the noun it modifies, *people*: *The two older people <u>standing over there</u> are Shelby's great-grandparents.*

The second word in the sentence, *State*, should be lower-cased; here it functions as a common noun, not as a proper noun.

FIND THE ERROR:

You have two choices: you can work overtime to finish the project, and you can tell your supervisor that you cannot meet the deadline.

FIND THE ERROR:

Alex plans to buy the most big cake he can find for his sister's birthday.

FIND THE ERROR:

Can you run to the grocery store tomorrow and pick up some milk and we need eggs, too.

The conjunction *and* should be changed to *or* to indicate a choice; as is, the sentence does not make sense.

The superlative form of the adjective *big* is *biggest*, not "most big."

This is a run-on sentence. It can be corrected in more than one way. Two examples: *Can you run to the grocery store tomorrow and pick up some milk and eggs? Can you run to the grocery store tomorrow and pick up some milk? We need eggs, too.*

FIND THE ERROR:

Only one among the school's 450 students were invited to enter the city's annual spelling bee.

FIND THE ERROR:

Thinking about all the happy and not-so-happy memories from my years in elementary and middle school.

FIND THE ERROR:

Here's what I'd like you to do, tidy up the living room, dust the furniture, and vacuum the rug.

The plural helping verb *were* does not agree with its singular subject, *one*. *Were* should be changed to *was*.

This is a sentence fragment. One way to complete the sentence might be the following: *That night, as was falling asleep, I started thinking about all the happy and not-so-happy memories from my years in elementary and middle school.*

The first comma in the sentence should be replaced with a colon (:).

FIND THE ERROR:

Almost all of the people in my family was planning to attend the reunion.

FIND THE ERROR:

There aunt is standing right over there with their parents.

Which words in the following sentence form an adjective phrase?

The woman on the bus wore a uniform.

The singular helping verb *was* does not agree with its plural subject, *people*. *Was* should be changed to *were*.

The first word, *There*, should be spelled *Their* to show possession.

"On the bus" is an adjective phrase that modifies the noun *woman*.

In the sentence *I threw the ball to Pablo*, which pronoun could you substitute for Pablo's name?

What are the main differences between adjectives and adverbs?

In the following sentence, identify one adverb and one adjective.

him

An adjective modifies a noun or a pronoun. Examples: *a gorgeous sunset*; *she is courageous*. An adverb modifies a verb, an adjective, or another adverb. Examples: *to amble lazily; amazingly beautiful; to speak incredibly quietly*.

Sleeping on the floor can be amazingly comfortable.
Adverb: *amazingly*; adjective: *comfortable*

Identify two misspelled words and spell them correctly.

Why didn't you tell me that your leaving on a two-week visit to you're grandmother?

Complete the following sentence with ONE pronoun.

I hope my grandparents will be in shape for their bicycle trip this summer—I don't want them to injure _____.

The seventh word, *your*, should be spelled *you're*. The second-to-last word, *you're*, should be spelled *your*.

themselves

7

WORD KNOWLEDGE

a, an

able, ible

without, not (*amoral*, *atheist*)

can happen (*audible*, *breakable*)

algia

alter

ambi

pain (*myalgia, neuralgia*)

other (*alternate, unaltered*)

both sides (*ambidextrous, ambivalent*)

ance, ancy

anthropo

anti

action, process (*defiance, tolerance*)

human (*anthropologist*)

against (*antibody, antibiotic*)

apert

auto

bene

open (*aperture*)

self (*autobiography*, *autograph*)

good, favorable (*benevolent*, *benefit*)

belli

bi, di

bio

war (*belligerent, bellicose*)

two (*binary, diatomic*)

life (*biology, biohazard*)

card

ced

cent

heart (*cardiology, cardiovascular*)

yield, go (*secede, intercede*)

one hundred (*century, percent*)

chrono

contra

cule

time (*chronology, chronological*)

counter (*contradict, contravene*)

very small (*molecule, minuscule*)

derm

dia

dict

skin (*dermatology*, *epidermis*)

across, through (*diameter*, *dialysis*)

to say (*dictation*, *predict*)

dom

dys

ectomy

quality (*wisdom*, *boredom*)

bad, hard (*dysfunctional*)

removal (*appendectomy*, *vasectomy*)

encephal

ex

fort

brain (*encephalitis*)

out, from (*external*, *exit*)

strength (*fortitude*, *effort*)

ful

gastro

geo

full of (*frightful, mouthful*)

stomach (*gastroenteritis, gastroenterology*)

earth (*geography*)

gram

graph

hetero

written (*epigram*, *grammatical*)

writing (*graphic*, *biography*)

different (*heterogenous*)

homo

hyper

hypo

same (*homogenous*)

above (*hyperactive, hyperventilate*)

below (*hypothermia, hypoglycemia*)

ice

ine

inter

condition, quality (*malice*, *avarice*)

nature of (*feminine*, *crystalline*)

between (*interstitial*, *interaction*)

iso

ist

itis

identical (*isometric, isosceles*)

one who (*cardiologist, specialist*)

inflammation (*appendicitis, hepatitis*)

ive

ject

macro

performs an action (*exhaustive*, *communicative*)

throw (*projection*, *eject*)

large (*macrophage*, *macroscopic*)

mal

ment

meter

bad (*malevolent, malnourished*)

act of, state of (*containment, alignment*)

measure (*thermometer, speedometer*)

micro

mono

mort

small (*micronutrient, microorganism*)

one, single (*monopoly, monogamy*)

death (*mortal, morgue*)

narco

neph

neuro

numbness, sleep (*narcotics, narcolepsy*)

kidney (*nephritis, nephrologist*)

nerve (*neurology, neuron*)

oid

osteo

peri

resembling (*fibroid, opioid*)

bone (*osteoporosis, osteoclast*)

around (*perineum, perimeter*)

port

pre

pseudo

carry (*transportation, portable*)

before (*preapproval, prefix*)

false (*pseudonym*)

rhino

rrhea

rupt

nose (*rhinoplasty, rhinoceros*)

flow, discharge (*amenorrhea, diarrhea*)

break (*disrupt, abrupt*)

sect

scope

tele

to cut (*dissect*, *sector*)

viewing instrument (*microscope*, *telescope*)

far off (*telephone*, *teleport*)

therm

un

heat (*thermal, thermometer*)

not (*unsafe, unwell*)

Made in the USA
Middletown, DE
19 April 2019